THE INFINITE GAME OF PRODUCT DEVELOPMENT

- ADARSH AGRAHARI

"Product development is a conversation with the user that doesn't really start till you launch"

– Paul Graham

Preface

This book is an exploration of the journey that product creators take when they choose to think beyond immediate wins and commit to building products that endure. It's about embracing an infinite mindset—one that values growth, adaptability, and meaningful impact over short-term gains. Whether you are a product manager, a designer, an entrepreneur, or anyone passionate about creating value, this book invites you to join an ongoing conversation about what it means to create products that truly matter.

The inspiration for this book came from my own experiences in product development, as well as from the countless conversations I've had with fellow product creators over the years. The lessons shared here are not just about building better products—they are about creating a better world through our work, our teams, and our commitment to an infinite journey of learning and growth.

I hope that by reading this book, you'll be inspired to think beyond the finite metrics that often dominate our work, to focus on the deeper impact you want to have, and to play the infinite game with curiosity, empathy, and resilience.

About the Author

Adarsh Agrahari is a seasoned product leader with a passion for building products that create meaningful, lasting impact. With years of experience in product development, Adarsh has worked across various industries, driving innovation and fostering growth. His approach to product management is deeply rooted in empathy, adaptability, and an infinite mindset — principles that guide his work and inspire those around him.

Adarsh's journey has been marked by a commitment to creating products that not only meet user needs but also contribute to a better world. He believes in the power of continuous learning, collaboration, and the importance of staying in the game — long after the first version is shipped. This book is a reflection of his experiences, insights, and the lessons learned from the many challenges and successes encountered along the way.

When he's not working on building impactful products, Adarsh enjoys mentoring aspiring product managers, exploring new ideas in technology, and contributing to the broader product community.

About the Book

The Infinite Game of Product Development is a call to all product creators to think beyond the immediate and embrace a mindset focused on long-term value and impact. This book redefines product development as an ongoing journey, one that values growth, adaptability, and meaningful contribution over short-term wins.

From shifting the focus from MVPs (Minimum Viable Products) to MLVs (Most Lovable Versions), to designing with empathy at the core, this book provides actionable insights and powerful stories to help you build products that endure. It delves into the importance of cultivating an infinite mindset in teams, balancing ambition with sustainable growth, and designing for humanity, not just users.

Whether you're a product manager, designer, entrepreneur, or someone who wants to create something that truly matters, *The Infinite Game of Product Development* offers a fresh perspective on what it takes to create products that last—products that evolve, inspire, and leave a legacy.
Join the journey of infinite product development and transform the way you build, innovate, and create.

Acknowledgements

Writing this book has been a journey that would not have been possible without the support and inspiration of countless individuals.

First and foremost, I want to express my deepest gratitude to the product creators and thinkers who have influenced my understanding of enduring products. Their relentless pursuit of meaningful work over empty growth has been a guiding light for this book.

To my team members, past and present: you have taught me the value of curiosity, resilience, and empathy. This book is as much yours as it is mine, and I am grateful for every conversation, challenge, and win we have experienced together.

To my mentors and peers in the product community: your wisdom and critiques have shaped the pages of this book. The late-night debates, the hard questions, and the visionary ideas pushed me to think beyond the obvious.

To my readers: thank you for choosing to spend your time with these pages. May this book inspire you to build products that matter—not just today, but for the generations to come.

Lastly, to my family and friends, whose patience and love have been my anchor through this journey: your unwavering belief in me gave me the courage to play the infinite game.

Thank you all for making this journey a truly infinite play.

Introduction: The Infinite Game of Product Development

Why Playing for the Long Term Matters

In a world that often celebrates short-term wins and rapid growth, playing the infinite game of product development requires a shift in mindset. The goal is not just to launch a product and move on but to create something that endures, evolves, and continues to provide value over time. It's about building a product that people love, trust, and rely on—a product that becomes a part of their lives in a meaningful way.

Playing for the long term matters because it allows us to focus on what truly drives impact. Instead of chasing quick metrics that look good on a quarterly report, we prioritize creating experiences that leave a lasting impression. We aim to solve real problems in ways that resonate deeply with our users, ensuring that our work has meaning beyond immediate gains.

When we adopt an infinite mindset, we stop seeing product development as a race to a finish line. Instead, it becomes a continuous journey — a series of steps toward a vision that grows and changes along with the world around us. This perspective encourages us to be patient, to think strategically, and to make decisions that prioritize sustainability and long-term success over short-term results.

Breaking Away from the Finite Mindset

Most traditional approaches to product development are rooted in a finite mindset. We set specific goals, define clear endpoints, and measure success by how quickly we can get there. While this approach works for certain projects, it often limits our ability to create products that are adaptable, resilient, and capable of enduring change.

Breaking away from the finite mindset means embracing ambiguity and being comfortable with the idea that the work is never truly done. Products are not static—they grow, evolve, and change in response to new technologies, shifting user needs, and emerging market trends. By letting go of the notion that there is a "final version" of our product, we open ourselves up to continuous improvement and innovation.

The finite mindset also tends to prioritize efficiency over exploration. We become focused on optimizing what already exists rather than questioning whether we're even building the right thing. Playing the infinite game means allowing space for exploration, experimentation, and even failure. It's about recognizing that the journey itself is valuable, and that the insights gained along the way are just as important as the final outcome.

To break away from the finite mindset, we need to redefine success. Instead of measuring our progress by how quickly we can ship a new feature or how many users we can acquire, we focus on the impact we're creating.

Are we making people's lives better? Are we solving real problems in ways that are meaningful and lasting? Are we creating something that can stand the test of time?

When we shift our focus from short-term wins to long-term impact, we begin to see product development not as a series of isolated projects but as an ongoing commitment to creating value. This is the essence of the infinite game: it's not about winning or losing — it's about staying in the game, continuously learning, growing, and evolving alongside our users and our products.

Chapter 1: Building for the Future — Today

Designing with Legacy in Mind

Building for the future is more than just delivering on immediate user needs — it's about laying a foundation that endures. As product creators, our responsibility is to design experiences that are both timely and timeless. We need to think about how our creations will evolve, how they will adapt, and how they will continue to serve users long after the initial launch.

Designing with legacy in mind means considering not just the features that users want today but also what they will need tomorrow. It's about imagining how the product might fit into people's lives years from now and how it could continue to create value. A well-designed product is not only functional; it also grows with its users, adapting to their changing needs without losing its core identity.

Take a moment to think of products that have endured for decades—those that have become part of our daily routines. They have one thing in common: they were built with a vision beyond immediate success. They anticipated change, embraced evolution, and stayed relevant by remaining flexible. This is the mindset we need to cultivate: one that sees the product not as a static entity but as a living, breathing experience that grows alongside its users.

Shifting from MVPs to MLVs (Most Lovable Versions)

In the world of product development, the concept of an MVP—Minimum Viable Product—has become ubiquitous. The idea is to launch quickly, learn, and iterate. But while MVPs have their place, they often focus too much on the minimum and not enough on what truly resonates with users.

Instead of aiming for the bare minimum, consider striving for the MLV—Most Lovable Version. An MLV doesn't just work; it delights. It's the version of the product that, while perhaps not feature-complete, captures the essence of what users will love about it. It's about finding that core experience that sparks joy, meets needs in a meaningful way, and leaves users wanting more.

The shift from MVP to MLV requires us to think deeply about the emotional journey of our users. What will make them smile? What will make their lives easier? What will make them say, "I can't imagine my life without this"? By focusing on what's lovable, rather than just what's viable, we create a product that forms an emotional connection—one that users will return to again and again.

This approach doesn't mean disregarding speed or iteration. It means being intentional about the first impression we create. It means understanding that the initial version of a product sets the tone for everything that follows. By making that first version lovable, we set ourselves up for long-term success, establishing a foundation on which we can build, refine, and grow.

Building for the future today is about making choices that prioritize longevity, adaptability, and love. It's about understanding that every decision we make today impacts the product's potential to endure. When we design with legacy in mind and strive for MLVs, we're not just creating products—we're creating experiences that matter, that endure, and that leave a lasting impact.

Chapter 2: The Art of Unlearning

Be stubborn on vision but flexible on details.
– Jeff Bezos

Shedding Outdated Beliefs

The process of unlearning is as important as learning itself. In product development, clinging to outdated beliefs and assumptions can hinder our ability to innovate and adapt. Shedding outdated beliefs requires us to question long-held assumptions about what users want, how products should be built, and what success looks like.

Unlearning is challenging because it involves letting go of what we know, which can feel uncomfortable and even threatening. But by recognizing that the world is constantly changing—and that our users' needs are evolving—we open ourselves up to new possibilities. We create space for growth, for reimagining how we build products, and for embracing new approaches that may be more effective in the present context.

To shed outdated beliefs, we must be willing to challenge our own thinking and to invite diverse perspectives into the conversation. It's about fostering a culture where questioning the status quo is encouraged, where curiosity is celebrated, and where learning is a continuous process.

Cultivating Beginner's Curiosity in Mature Teams

One of the greatest challenges for mature teams is maintaining the curiosity and openness that define beginner's mind. As teams grow more experienced, there is a natural tendency to become more rigid in thinking, to rely on established processes, and to become resistant to change. However, cultivating beginner's curiosity is essential for innovation.

Beginner's curiosity is about approaching problems with fresh eyes, even when we've encountered similar challenges before. It's about asking questions like, "What if we did it differently?" or "Is there a better way?" It's about being open to ideas that may seem unconventional or risky, and being willing to experiment without the fear of failure.

Mature teams can cultivate beginner's curiosity by embracing a culture of experimentation, where trying new things is seen as a path to learning rather than as a risk to be avoided. Leaders play a crucial role in this by modeling curiosity, encouraging exploration, and creating an environment where team members feel safe to take risks and share new ideas.

By shedding outdated beliefs and cultivating beginner's curiosity, teams can remain adaptable, innovative, and responsive to the changing needs of users. This is the art of unlearning—letting go of what no longer serves us and making space for what will.

Always have empathy for your customers."

– Jesse Owens II, Product Director of Digital Payments at MasterCard

Chapter 3: Embracing Uncertainty

The Role of Adaptability in Product Success

In the ever-changing landscape of product development, adaptability is one of the most critical factors for success. Markets change, technologies evolve, and user needs shift—often in unpredictable ways. The ability to adapt to these changes, to pivot when necessary, and to adjust our approach based on new information is what sets successful products apart from those that fail to keep up.

Adaptability means being open to change and being willing to adjust course when the situation demands it. It's about recognizing that our initial assumptions may not always be correct, and that the path to success is rarely a straight line. Adaptable teams are those that can respond quickly to new challenges, learn from setbacks, and use those lessons to improve.

Adaptability also involves a willingness to listen to users, to understand their changing needs, and to evolve the product accordingly. It's about being flexible in our thinking and recognizing that what worked yesterday may not work tomorrow. By embracing adaptability, we ensure that our products remain relevant, valuable, and capable of meeting the needs of our users in a dynamic environment.

Navigating Complexity with Vision and Agility

Product development is inherently complex. There are countless variables to consider, from user needs and market trends to technical challenges and team dynamics. Navigating this complexity requires both vision and agility.

Vision provides us with a sense of direction—a clear understanding of what we are trying to achieve and why it matters. It's the guiding star that helps us make decisions, prioritize efforts, and stay focused on the bigger picture. Without vision, we risk getting lost in the details and losing sight of what truly matters.

Agility, on the other hand, is what allows us to respond to changes and navigate the unexpected twists and turns of product development. It's about being flexible, iterative, and willing to adjust our approach based on new information. Agility enables us to move quickly, to experiment, and to learn from both successes and failures.

When we combine vision with agility, we are able to navigate complexity with confidence. We have a clear sense of where we are headed, but we are also open to adjusting our course as needed. This balance between vision and agility is what allows us to embrace uncertainty, to thrive in the face of complexity, and to create products that are both innovative and resilient.

If you keep your eye on the profit, you're going to skimp on the product. But if you focus on making really great products, then the profits will follow."

– Steve Jobs, former CEO of Apple

Chapter 4: Human-Centered Resilience

Designing with Empathy at the Core

Human-centered design is about putting people at the center of everything we create. It's about understanding the needs, desires, and challenges of our users and designing products that genuinely improve their lives. At the core of human-centered resilience is empathy—the ability to see the world through the eyes of our users and to design solutions that address their real needs.

Empathy allows us to go beyond surface-level solutions and to create products that resonate on a deeper level. It's about understanding not just what users say they want, but also what they truly need. It's about listening, observing, and putting ourselves in their shoes to gain a deeper understanding of their experiences.

By designing with empathy, we create products that are not only functional but also meaningful. We build trust with our users by showing that we understand their challenges and that we are committed to solving them. This trust is the foundation of human-centered resilience—products that users rely on, return to, and advocate for because they feel understood and supported.

Fostering Trust Between Products and Users

Trust is one of the most important factors in the success of any product. Without trust, users are unlikely to engage deeply with a product, to share their data, or to become loyal advocates. Fostering trust requires us to be transparent, reliable, and consistent in our actions.

Trust is built over time through every interaction a user has with a product. It's about delivering on promises, being honest about what the product can and cannot do, and ensuring that users feel safe and supported. It's about respecting their privacy, providing clear communication, and being responsive to their needs.

Human-centered resilience is about creating products that users can depend on—products that are designed not just to function well but to foster a sense of trust and connection. By prioritizing empathy and trust, we create products that are resilient in the face of change, adaptable to user needs, and capable of making a lasting impact in people's lives.

"Your most unhappy customers are your greatest source of learning."

– Bill Gates, Microsoft

Chapter 5: Infinite vs. Finite Success Metrics

Moving Beyond Vanity Metrics

In the pursuit of product success, it's easy to get caught up in vanity metrics—those numbers that look impressive on paper but don't necessarily reflect meaningful progress. Metrics like user acquisition, page views, or downloads can provide a sense of achievement, but they often fail to capture the true value a product is delivering.

Moving beyond vanity metrics means focusing on metrics that matter—those that reflect the real impact we are having on our users' lives. Are we solving meaningful problems? Are we improving user satisfaction? Are we creating lasting value? These are the questions we need to ask ourselves.

Meaningful metrics are those that align with our long-term vision and that provide insight into how well we are meeting the needs of our users. They help us understand whether we are creating a product that people love, that they find valuable, and that they want to use again and again.

Measuring Impact, Happiness, and Contribution

To truly understand the success of a product, we need to look beyond traditional metrics and consider the broader impact we are having. Are we making our users' lives better? Are we contributing to their happiness, productivity, or well-being? Are we creating something that has a positive impact on the world?

Measuring impact means considering the qualitative aspects of our product's success. It means gathering feedback from users, understanding their experiences, and looking at how our product fits into their lives. It means considering not just the numbers, but the stories behind those numbers — the real people whose lives are being affected by what we create.

Happiness is a powerful metric because it speaks to the emotional connection users have with our product. It's about creating experiences that delight, that solve real problems, and that leave users feeling better off. By focusing on impact, happiness, and contribution, we ensure that our products are not just successful in the short term, but that they have a lasting, positive effect on the world.

"Building a good customer experience does not happen by accident. It happens by design."

– Clare Muscutt, Founder and Director at CXMperience

Chapter 6: Crafting Teams for the Long Haul

Developing an Infinite Mindset in Teams

Building products that endure requires teams that are committed to the long game. Developing an infinite mindset in teams means fostering a culture that values learning, growth, and long-term impact over short-term wins. It's about encouraging team members to think beyond immediate goals and to consider the broader vision of what they are creating.

An infinite mindset is one that embraces curiosity, resilience, and adaptability. It's about being willing to learn from failure, to iterate, and to keep moving forward even when faced with challenges. It's about understanding that the work we do today is part of a larger journey — a journey that is focused on creating value that endures.

Leaders play a key role in developing an infinite mindset in their teams. By setting a clear vision, encouraging collaboration, and creating an environment where experimentation is valued, leaders can inspire their teams to think beyond the present moment and to focus on the long-term impact of their work.

Balancing Ambition with Sustainable Growth

Ambition is an important driver of innovation and progress, but it must be balanced with sustainable growth. Pushing too hard, too fast can lead to burnout, poor decision-making, and products that fail to deliver on their promises. Sustainable growth means setting a pace that allows for learning, reflection, and continuous improvement.

Balancing ambition with sustainable growth requires us to be mindful of our team's well-being, to prioritize quality over speed, and to recognize that creating something meaningful takes time. It's about setting realistic expectations, celebrating progress, and understanding that the journey is just as important as the destination.

By fostering an infinite mindset and balancing ambition with sustainability, we create teams that are capable of enduring the ups and downs of product development—teams that are resilient, motivated, and committed to creating products that stand the test of time.

Any damn fool can make something complex, it takes a genius to make something simple."

– Pete Seeger, Product Director at Docusign

Chapter 7: The Beauty of Evolution—Iteration as a Journey

Treating Each Version as a Living Entity

Product development is not a one-time event—it's a continuous journey of iteration, improvement, and evolution. Each version of a product is a living entity, one that grows and changes in response to user feedback, market conditions, and technological advancements.

Treating each version as a living entity means recognizing that our work is never truly done. It means embracing the idea that each release is an opportunity to learn, to refine, and to move closer to our vision. It means being open to change, to experimentation, and to the idea that our product will continue to evolve over time.

This mindset allows us to approach product development with a sense of curiosity and excitement. Each version is a chance to make the product better, to solve new problems, and to delight our users in new ways. By treating each version as a living entity, we create a product that is dynamic, adaptable, and capable of growing alongside its users.

Continuous Growth as a Product Principle

Continuous growth is at the heart of the infinite game. It's about always looking for ways to improve, to add value, and to create something that is better than what came before. Continuous growth means being committed to learning, to experimenting, and to pushing the boundaries of what is possible.

As product creators, we must embrace the idea that growth is not linear — it's a journey of ups and downs, of successes and setbacks. It's about being willing to take risks, to learn from failure, and to keep moving forward. By making continuous growth a core principle of our work, we ensure that our products are always evolving, always improving, and always capable of meeting the needs of our users.

At the heart of every product person, there's a desire to make someone's life easier or simpler. If we listen to the customer and give them what they need, they'll reciprocate with love and loyalty to your brand."

– Francis Brown, Product Development Manager at Alaska Airlines

Chapter 8: Purpose and Profit—Not a Trade-off

Finding the Intersection of Purpose and Sustainability

For too long, purpose and profit have been seen as opposing forces. But the truth is, they are not mutually exclusive. In fact, the most successful products are often those that find the intersection of purpose and sustainability — those that create value for users while also contributing to the greater good.

Finding this intersection requires us to think deeply about why we are building what we are building. What is the purpose of our product? What impact do we want to have on the world? How can we create something that is not only profitable but also meaningful?

When we build with purpose, we create products that resonate with users on a deeper level. We create experiences that go beyond functionality and that connect with users' values, aspirations, and needs. By finding the intersection of purpose and sustainability, we ensure that our products are not just successful in the short term, but that they have a lasting, positive impact on the world.

Stories of Products that Endure and Thrive

There are countless examples of products that have endured and thrived because they were built with purpose. These are products that have not only met the needs of their users but have also contributed to the greater good — products that have made a positive impact on society, on the environment, and on the lives of the people who use them.

By studying these stories, we can learn valuable lessons about what it takes to create products that endure. We can learn about the importance of staying true to our values, of being willing to adapt and evolve, and of always keeping our users at the center of everything we do. These stories remind us that purpose and profit are not a trade-off — they are two sides of the same coin.

"At the end of the day, your job isn't to get the requirements right – your job is to change the world."

– Jeff Patton, Veteran Product Manager and Consultant

Chapter 9: The Art of Letting Go

Knowing When to Pivot or Sunset a Product

In the world of product development, not every idea will succeed. Knowing when to pivot or sunset a product is an important skill for any product creator. It's about recognizing when a product is no longer meeting the needs of its users, when the market has changed, or when the original vision is no longer viable.

Letting go of a product can be difficult, especially when we have invested time, energy, and passion into its creation. But sometimes, letting go is the best way to create space for new ideas, for new opportunities, and for growth. It's about being honest with ourselves, with our users, and with our teams about what is working and what is not.

Pivoting is not a failure—it's a recognition that the path we are on may not be the right one, and that there is a better way forward. Sunsetting a product is not an end—it's a chance to learn, to reflect, and to apply those lessons to future endeavors. By embracing the art of letting go, we create space for innovation, for new possibilities, and for the next chapter of our journey.

Ensuring Legacy Even in Closure

Even when a product is sunsetted, its legacy can endure. Ensuring legacy means taking the time to reflect on what worked, what didn't, and what lessons can be carried forward. It's about celebrating the successes, learning from the challenges, and finding ways to apply those lessons to future products.

Ensuring legacy also means considering the impact on users. How can we make the transition as smooth as possible? How can we ensure that users feel supported, respected, and valued, even as we move on from a product? By focusing on the legacy we leave behind, we ensure that our work has a lasting impact, even in closure.

"Customer love means two sides of the same coin to me. On one side is knowing your customer and building fantastic experiences for them. Your dedication and passion to making their life easier and delighting them feeds into the other side. When approached this way, not only will you have a loyal user base, they will also be your strongest advocates and critics."

– Andrew Wang, Senior Product Manager at Gap

Chapter 10: Designing for Humanity, Not Just Users

How Products Shape Culture

Products are not just tools — they are part of the culture we live in. They shape the way we communicate, the way we work, and the way we interact with the world. Designing for humanity means recognizing the broader impact our products have on society and taking responsibility for that impact.

Products have the power to bring people together, to solve meaningful problems, and to create positive change. But they also have the potential to create harm, to exclude, or to reinforce negative behaviors. As product creators, we have a responsibility to consider the cultural impact of what we create and to design with humanity in mind.

By designing for humanity, we create products that are inclusive, that empower users, and that contribute to a better world. We think beyond individual features and consider the broader implications of our work. We recognize that our products are part of a larger ecosystem, and we take responsibility for the impact they have on that ecosystem.

Focusing on Impact Over Consumption

In a world that often values consumption above all else, focusing on impact is a powerful shift. It's about creating products that are not just designed to be used, but that are designed to make a positive impact on the lives of their users. It's about thinking beyond the metrics of engagement and usage and considering the real difference our products are making.

Focusing on impact means designing for long-term value rather than short-term gains. It means prioritizing quality over quantity, and creating experiences that are meaningful, that solve real problems, and that leave users better off. By focusing on impact over consumption, we create products that are not only successful but also valuable, enduring, and capable of making a positive difference in the world.

"Customers are who we build our apps for, so we want to give them what they want and need while empathizing with their struggles and frustrations. For me, it's not necessarily the mantra of the customer is always right, but do everything with the customer in mind."

– Jason Pace, Software Engineering Manager at Alchemer Mobile (formerly Apptentive)

Chapter 11: The Infinite Play Begins with You

A Call to Action for Product Creators

The infinite game of product development is not just about the products we create—it's about the mindset we bring to our work. It's about being committed to the long game, to creating value that endures, and to making a positive impact on the world. As product creators, we have the power to shape the future, to create products that matter, and to leave a lasting legacy.

This is a call to action for all product creators: to embrace the infinite game, to think beyond immediate wins, and to focus on the long-term impact of our work. It's about being willing to learn, to grow, and to evolve alongside our users and our products. It's about staying in the game, continuously improving, and always striving to create something better.

Embracing the Infinite Play in Life and Work

The principles of the infinite game apply not only to product development but also to life. Embracing the infinite play means approaching our work, our relationships, and our personal growth with a sense of curiosity, resilience, and openness. It means being willing to learn, to adapt, and to keep moving forward, even when faced with challenges.

In life, as in product development, the journey is just as important as the destination. It's about finding joy in the process, about being open to new experiences, and about making a positive impact on the world around us. By embracing the infinite play in both life and work, we create a legacy that endures—a legacy of growth, of impact, and of continuous improvement.

"If you are not embarrassed by the first version of your product, you've launched too late."

– Reid Garrett Hoffman, Entrepreneur

Conclusion: The Legacy We Leave Behind

Reflections on Long-Term Impact

As product creators, we have the opportunity to shape the future, to create products that matter, and to make a lasting impact on the world. The legacy we leave behind is not just about the products we create—it's about the values we uphold, the people we touch, and the difference we make.

Long-term impact is about creating something that endures, that continues to provide value, and that makes a positive difference in the lives of our users. It's about focusing on what truly matters, on solving real problems, and on creating experiences that resonate on a deep level. By keeping our focus on long-term impact, we ensure that our work is meaningful, valuable, and capable of making a positive difference in the world.

The Endless Iteration of a Better World

The infinite game of product development is about more than just creating products—it's about creating a better world. It's about using our skills, our creativity, and our passion to solve meaningful problems, to empower users, and to contribute to a better future.

The work is never truly done. There is always more to learn, more to create, and more to improve. But by embracing the infinite play, by committing to the long game, and by focusing on the impact we want to have, we can create products that endure, that inspire, and that leave a lasting legacy. The iteration of a better world is endless—and it begins with each of us.

Glossary

- **Infinite Mindset**: A perspective that prioritizes long-term value, adaptability, and continuous growth over short-term wins and finite goals.
- **Minimum Viable Product (MVP)**: The simplest version of a product that can be released to test an idea or concept and gather user feedback.
- **Most Lovable Version (MLV)**: A version of a product that captures the essence of what users will love, focusing on delight and emotional connection rather than just viability.
- **Human-Centered Design**: An approach to product design that puts the needs, desires, and challenges of users at the core of the creation process.
- **Vanity Metrics**: Metrics that may look impressive but do not necessarily reflect meaningful progress or impact, such as page views or download numbers.
- **Sustainable Growth**: Growth that is balanced and paced in a way that ensures long-term success without compromising quality or well-being.

- **Empathy**: The ability to understand and share the feelings of others, used in product development to create meaningful and user-centered experiences.

Practical Toolkit for Human-Centered Design

To help teams embrace human-centered design, use the following toolkit to ensure that empathy remains at the core of your product development process:

1. **User Personas**: Develop detailed user personas based on real research. Include motivations, needs, frustrations, and behaviors. These personas should represent your primary user groups, making it easier for your team to focus on solving specific problems for real people.

2. **Empathy Mapping**: Conduct empathy mapping workshops with your team to better understand the emotional journey of your users. Create a visual representation that answers questions like: What does the user think? What do they feel? What are their biggest challenges? Empathy maps help build a shared understanding of your users.

3. **User Journey Mapping**: Visualize the user journey from start to finish. Identify touchpoints, moments of friction, and opportunities for delight. A well-designed journey map can help you see the big picture and understand where improvements are needed.

4. **Field Research**: Engage with users directly through interviews, surveys, and observational studies. First-hand insights are crucial for understanding the real context in which your product is used. Field research can often uncover pain points and needs that were not captured during earlier phases of development.

5. **Prototyping and Testing**: Create low-fidelity prototypes to test with users early and often. Invite feedback on how well the prototype addresses their needs and if it's solving the right problems. Iterating on these prototypes based on user input ensures that your product evolves according to what truly matters to your audience.

6. **Daily Stand-Ups and User Stories**: Use daily stand-ups to keep empathy top of mind. Start or end each stand-up with a user story that reflects why the current work is important to your users. Keeping these stories front and center can help teams stay aligned on the goal of creating meaningful solutions.

7. **Walk in Their Shoes**: Encourage team members to "walk in the users' shoes" by using the product as intended. Experiencing your product from the user's perspective can reveal pain points that might have been overlooked during design.

8. **Customer Feedback Loops**: Set up regular customer feedback sessions where you hear directly from users about their experience. These feedback loops are valuable for understanding what works well and where improvements are needed. Listening to users fosters continuous empathy throughout the development process.

9. **Design Sprints**: Run design sprints to tackle challenging problems with a focused, collaborative effort. By bringing together team members from different disciplines to work intensively over a few days, you can rapidly prototype and validate solutions with real users.

10. **Accessibility Reviews**: Assess the accessibility of your product to ensure it meets the needs of all users, including those with disabilities. Ensuring accessibility is an important aspect of human-centered design that promotes inclusivity and user satisfaction.

Case Studies

Case Study 1: The Evolution of Slack - From MVP to MLV

Slack started as an internal tool for a gaming company and quickly evolved into one of the most beloved communication platforms in the world. Initially released as an MVP, Slack focused on solving real problems that teams faced with workplace communication. By listening to user feedback and continuously improving the product, Slack moved from an MVP to an MLV (Most Lovable Version) that resonates deeply with its audience. Slack's journey shows how focusing on the core emotional and functional needs of users can create a product that not only works but delights.

Case Study 2: Netflix's Adaptability - Thriving Through Market Shifts

Netflix started as a DVD rental company but evolved into a leading streaming platform, adapting to market trends and consumer behavior. Their journey highlights the importance of adaptability and vision. By investing in streaming technology early on, even when it seemed like a risky move, Netflix positioned itself to dominate the future of entertainment. This case study exemplifies how embracing uncertainty and adapting to changing circumstances can be pivotal in ensuring long-term success.

Case Study 3: Patagonia's Purpose-Driven Growth

Patagonia is a brand that has successfully integrated purpose into profit, proving that the two are not mutually exclusive. By focusing on sustainability and environmental advocacy, Patagonia has built a loyal customer base that supports the company's mission. This case study shows how purpose-driven growth can create a lasting impact while also achieving profitability. It also demonstrates that products that align with values and a higher purpose can connect deeply with their audience.

Reflection Exercises

Reflection Exercise 1: Designing for the Long Term

Think about your current product or project. Are you designing with legacy in mind? Write down three ways you could change your approach today to ensure that your product remains valuable years into the future.

Reflection Exercise 2: Breaking Away from the Finite Mindset

Identify one area in your product development process where a finite mindset might be limiting your potential. How can you shift to an infinite mindset that encourages exploration, experimentation, and long-term thinking?

Reflection Exercise 3: Cultivating Beginner's Curiosity

Reflect on a recent project or problem your team faced. How did your team approach it? Was there room for curiosity and exploration? Write down three questions you could have asked to cultivate a beginner's mindset.

Reflection Exercise 4: Measuring What Truly Matters

Review the metrics you are currently using to track your product's success. Are they vanity metrics or do they reflect real impact? Write down three meaningful metrics that align with your product's long-term vision.

Think about how your product aligns with a higher purpose. How does your product benefit your users and the broader community? Write down three ways you can ensure that your product not only drives profit but also contributes positively to society.

Appendix

Next Monday Morning Execution Template

The goal of this template is to help you turn the insights from *The Infinite Game of Product Development* into actionable steps. Use it each Monday morning to set clear intentions and prioritize tasks that align with the infinite mindset.

Step 1: Reflect on the Long-Term Vision
- What is your long-term vision for the product? Write it down and ensure that all tasks this week contribute to that vision.

Step 2: Set Weekly Objectives
- Identify three key objectives that align with your long-term vision.
  - Objective 1:
  - Objective 2:
  - Objective 3:

Step 3: Embrace an Infinite Mindset
- Identify one area of your work that you can approach with an infinite mindset. How can you prioritize sustainability and adaptability?
  - Infinite Mindset Focus for This Week:

Step 4: Cultivate Empathy
- List two ways to put your users at the center of your work this week. How will you connect with your users or better understand their needs?
  - Empathy Action 1:
  - Empathy Action 2:

Step 5: Iterate with Purpose
- What iteration can you make to improve the product this week? How can you make the current version more lovable?
  - Iteration Focus for the Week:

Step 6: Reflect on Metrics that Matter
- Identify one metric that truly reflects the impact of your work. How will you measure it this week?
  - Impact Metric for the Week:

Step 7: Engage Your Team
- How can you inspire your team with the infinite mindset? List one activity or discussion topic to encourage your team to think long term.
  - Team Engagement Plan:

Step 8: Evaluate and Adjust
- At the end of the week, evaluate your progress. What worked well, and what could be improved? How will you adjust next week's focus?